A TRUE BOOK™

D0796572

The Connecticut Colony

KEVIN CUNNINGHAM

Children's Press®
An Imprint of Scholastic Inc.
New York Toronto London Auckland Sydney
Mexico City New Delhi Hong Kong
Danbury, Connecticut

Content Consultant

Jeffrey Kaja, PhD
Associate Professor of History
California State University, Northridge

Library of Congress Cataloging-in-Publication Data

Cunningham, Kevin, 1966–
   The Connecticut colony/Kevin Cunningham.
      p. cm.—(A true book)
   Includes bibliographical references and index.
   ISBN-13: 978-0-531-25387-8 (lib. bdg.)   ISBN-13: 978-0-531-26600-7 (pbk.)
   ISBN-10: 0-531-25387-2 (lib. bdg.)   ISBN-10: 0-531-26600-1 (pbk.)
   1. Connecticut—History—Colonial period, ca. 1600–1775—Juvenile literature. 2. Connecticut—
History—Revolution, 1775–1783—Juvenile literature. I. Title. II. Series.
   F97.C876 2011
   974.6'02—dc22   2011009487

All rights reserved. Published in 2012 by Children's Press, an imprint of Scholastic Inc.
Printed in China 62
SCHOLASTIC, CHILDREN'S PRESS, A TRUE BOOK, and associated logos are trademarks and/or registered trademarks of Scholastic Inc.
6 7 8 9 10 R 21 20 19 18 17

Find the Truth!

Everything you are about to read is true *except* for one of the sentences on this page.

Which one is **TRUE**?

T or F   Connecticut wrote a constitution as early as 1639.

T or F   Everyone in Connecticut agreed to fight the Revolutionary War against Britain.

Find the answers in this book.

Contents

Jonathan Trumbull

THE **BIG** TRUTH!

Connecticut's Founding Fathers

Colonists argue with King Charles II.

How did these founders help
American independence? **38**

According to legend, Joseph Wadsworth hid Connecticut's colonial charter in an oak tree.

5

Timeline of Connecticut Colony History

About 10,000 B.C.E.

Early Native Americans settle present-day Connecticut and the surrounding areas.

1633

The first permanent European settlement in Connecticut is established.

1639

The Fundamental Orders are written.

1775

American colonists fight first battles with the British.

1788

Connecticut ratifies the U.S. Constitution.

CHAPTER 1

Native American Life

Around 16 Native American peoples settled in modern-day Connecticut thousands of years before it was colonized by Europeans. These native peoples lived in different groups. But they shared similar languages and customs. Most made their homes along nearby bodies of water. Each group claimed a territory. They set up small villages near the coast in the summer. They spent winters in forest valleys. These valleys provided plenty of trees for firewood.

Farms, Fish, and Furs

Women planted fields of maize (corn), beans, and squash around the summer villages. They also gathered seafood such as clams at the shore. Men hunted waterbirds in the marshes. They canoed into the ocean to catch fish with spears and nets. The men hunted deer, bears, foxes, and beavers during the winter. The animals provided meat. They also provided skins and furs for clothing. People turned animal bone and antler into tools.

This modern-day recreation shows what the inside of a traditional Pequot lodge might have looked like.

Women usually took charge of things around the home, including farming.

A wigwam's design enabled it to be put up and taken down quickly.

Movable House

Connecticut native peoples usually lived in a **wigwam**. Wigwams were domed structures made of bark, mud, and grass built onto a wooden frame. Women packed up the wigwam cover when it came time to move. They left the frame standing for use the next year. Family members stretched out animal skins inside the wigwam for use as beds. A cooking fire in the center of the wigwam provided light and heat.

miles 0 20

km 0 20

Colonial boundaries

Area enlarged

Original 13 Colonies

MASSACHUSETTS

NEW YORK

East Granby

Windsor

Hartford

Wethersfield

Farmington R.

Connecticut River

NIPMUC

Quinebaug River

RHODE ISLAND

PODUNK

Watertown

CONNECTICUT

PEQUOT

Naugatuck River

Quinnipiac R.

MOHEGAN

Thames R.

NIANTIC

Housatonic River

Danbury

New Haven

Saybrook

New London

Groton

Block Island

Long Island Sound

Greenwich

Long Island

ATLANTIC OCEAN

CHAPTER 2

The Europeans Arrive

Dutch trader Adriaen Block bought furs from Native Americans near present-day New York City in 1613. Block lost his ship in a fire. The natives helped him and his men survive the winter. The Indians and sailors built a boat called the *Onrust*. This name meant "restless" in Dutch. Block sailed his ship up the Quinnehtukqut River to where the Saukiog people lived. Block heard the natives' name for the river. He spelled it *Connecticut*. *Quinnehtukqut* means "place of the long river" in Mohegan.

The arrival of Adriaen Block and other Europeans introduced unfamiliar diseases to native populations.

Diseases Bring Disaster

Diseases had killed thousands of Native Americans in villages from Long Island Sound to Maine within two years of Block's journey. Ships from Europe had recently sailed to other lands. The Europeans picked up diseases on their journeys and carried them to the Americas. Diseases such as smallpox were passed from one native group to another. Only about 6,000 to 7,000 native people remained in the Connecticut region by the time the **epidemic** ended.

First European Settlements

The Pilgrims were a group of religious outcasts fleeing **prejudice** in England. They founded Plymouth Plantation in Massachusetts in 1620. A small band of Pilgrims started a new settlement along the Quinnehtukqut River in 1633. The settlers built a house near the river. They erected a wall of wooden stakes around it. This gave them protection against attacks by Native Americans and Dutch traders. They named the settlement Windsor. It was soon surrounded by farms.

Settlers originally called the Windsor settlement Dorchester.

One hundred people settled at Windsor in its first year. Despite bad winters, more settlers continued to join them. The nearby settlement of Wethersfield had a population of 800 within a few years. One hundred people settled at Hartford. The three towns formed the Connecticut **Colony** in April 1636. The colonial leaders passed laws that forbade the sale of guns and liquor to Native Americans.

The first Hartford settlers came from present-day Cambridge, Massachusetts.

Pequots flee a burning village during the Pequot War in 1637.

The Pequot War

The settlers battled the Pequot from 1636 to 1638. The Pequot were the most powerful local natives. The fighting ended when the Connecticut **militia** trapped more than 600 Pequot in a burning village near Narragansett Harbor. The surviving Pequot fled. But militiamen tracked them down. The Indians were either killed or sold into slavery.

A Constitution

The colony's leaders wrote the Fundamental Orders in 1639. This was a **constitution** that outlined the duties of the government. The Fundamental Orders allowed colonists to vote for a **legislature** and a governor. Only adult male property owners had the right to vote.

But choosing one's own leaders was a groundbreaking idea at the time.

The Fundamental Orders united the Windsor, Hartford, and Wethersfield settlements.

In Need of a Charter

John Winthrop, Jr., was elected governor of Connecticut in 1657 and 1659.

About 1,000 settlers lived in the Connecticut Colony at the end of the Pequot War. New waves of settlers founded New Haven and other towns soon after the war. Connecticut's population had grown to nearly 8,000 by 1660. But the colonists had no **legal** right to settle there. The Dutch or another country could seize their land. Colonial governor John Winthrop, Jr., went to England in 1662. He asked the king for a **charter** to make Connecticut an English colony under English protection.

Challenges Continue

Connecticut overcame several new threats throughout the late 1600s. Metacomet was chief of the Wampanoag peoples. He went to war against Massachusetts colonists in 1675. His warriors burned homes in the Connecticut towns of Granby and Simsbury the next year. The conflict ended when Metacomet died. England's King Charles II had given half of Connecticut to the colony of New York by then.

Metacomet, also called King Philip, led the Wampanoag during King Philip's War against the colonists.

18

The oak in which the Connecticut charter was supposedly hidden became known as the Charter Oak.

The Hidden Charter Trick

King James II combined Connecticut with other English colonies in 1686 to form the Dominion of New England. New England's governor was Edmund Andros. He wanted to control the legislature. He demanded that each colony turn over its charter to him. According to legend, Hartford's leaders hid the Connecticut charter in an oak tree. Andros still took charge. But the Dominion split apart in 1688 when King James II was overthrown.

CHAPTER 3

Farmhouses and Schoolhouses

About 90 percent of Connecticut's people lived on farms and grew crops such as maize, peas, and tobacco during the colony's early history. Fishers hauled fish out of Long Island Sound. Whalers hunting in the Atlantic Ocean brought back whale oil for lamps and whalebone for umbrellas and clothing. But even on the coast, where fishers and whalers worked, farms usually surrounded the towns.

 Connecticut farms often kept cows, pigs, and horses.

Farmwork

Early colonial families worked hard. Every member did his or her part to help with chores. Men and boys got up before sunrise to chop wood and dig ditches. They plowed and planted the fields in the spring. They picked the crops in autumn. Farmers sold the food not needed by the family in town markets. They also traded for products such as glass, guns, and metal tools.

Reenacters now work on some historic colonial farms.

A colonial farmer could plant an acre in a day.

"Land of Steady Habits"

Most early settlers in Connecticut had Puritan beliefs. The Puritans practiced a strict type of Christianity. The father was the dominant figure in the family. Adults and children all worked long hours six days a week. Families attended church from Saturday evening to Sunday evening. Puritans expected everyone to live modest lives. Their ways earned Connecticut the nickname Land of Steady Habits.

Puritans gather for their first Sunday religious service in present-day New Haven, before their church building was built.

Women and girls also worked long hours. They cooked and spun wool into yarn. They also made and mended clothing. Women sealed vegetables and fruits in jars in the fall for use during the winter. Families preserved meat by drying and salting it. The women also used herbs and other home medicines to treat illnesses because few physicians lived in the colony.

The women in a family kept busy all day long cooking, baking, churning butter, spinning yarn, and sewing and mending clothing.

Puritans felt that religious study was an important part of education. →

Colonial Childhood

Children walked to the nearest town to attend school after finishing morning chores. Connecticut had passed a law early in its history stating that any town with at least 50 families must open a schoolhouse. One teacher taught children of all ages in a one-room building. Students learned reading, writing, and math. Teachers kept strict rules. Students were hit on the knuckles with a wooden stick if they misbehaved.

Very few colonial children attended school past eighth grade. Teenagers were expected to work instead. Boys often worked in towns as unpaid **apprentices**. A tradesman taught an apprentice a skill such as barrel making or carpentry. Girls usually stayed home and learned sewing, cooking, and other skills from their mothers. Storekeepers, lawyers, shipbuilders, and many other skilled professionals began to settle in the towns as the 1700s continued.

A person who created the metal letters used by printers for newspapers, books, or other publications was called a type founder.

Ethan Allen's furnace was used to produce more than 800 cannonballs during the Revolutionary War.

Manufacturing

Connecticut was one of the few colonies that built factories. Factories using waterwheels for power sprang up along Connecticut's rivers around 1750. Hats made in Wethersfield and clocks manufactured in Windsor were sold in other American colonies and England. Future American Revolutionary War hero Ethan Allen helped build a furnace that melted iron for cannons. Connecticut would soon need such weapons.

British ships sail along the coast as British soldiers take over a French fort in Quebec.

The French and Indian War extended into the area that became present-day Canada.

CHAPTER 4

The Road to Independence

France and Great Britain both claimed the Ohio River region in western Pennsylvania in 1754. The French began to build forts. British and colonial troops marched west to stop them. One group was led by a young officer named George Washington. Washington clashed twice with French soldiers. The small battles touched off the French and Indian War. This war is also known as the Seven Years' War.

War With France

France and its Native American allies defeated British and colonial troops in battle after battle for the next four years. No fighting took place in Connecticut. But the colony's militia took part in battles in New York and Massachusetts. The British had pushed toward the important French city of Montreal in Canada by 1758. Soldiers under Connecticut officer Israel Putnam captured two French ships in 1760. Britain took control of the city and won the war.

Israel Putnam helped organize the Sons of Liberty.

Paul Revere scatters leaflets for the Sons of Liberty.

Paying for Victory

The years of fighting drove the British government into **debt**. Parliament, Britain's legislature, decided to tax the American colonies to raise money. The 1765 Stamp Act forced colonists to pay for a government stamp on printed material such as licenses and newspapers. Angry colonists protested the tax and refused to buy British goods. A secret anti-British group called the Sons of Liberty organized throughout the American colonies.

Parliament eliminated the Stamp Act. But it soon imposed taxes on paint, paper, tea, and many other products. Protests and refusals to buy British products forced Parliament to drop many of the taxes. But the tax on tea remained. A new law allowed a British company to sell its tea for less than American companies could sell it for. Colonists protested by refusing to let boats full of tea unload in colonial ports.

Some American colonists spun wool for cloth to avoid buying British-made clothing.

British ships surround Boston Harbor in Massachusetts in 1773.

In Boston, Massachusetts, a Sons of Liberty group threw a boatload of British tea into Boston Harbor. Britain responded by closing the harbor. No shipments came in or out of port. The colonists' businesses suffered. There was a shortage of food. Connecticut colonists sneaked fish, maize, and other supplies into the city. Representatives from 12 of the 13 colonies met in Philadelphia at the First Continental Congress in September 1774 to decide what to do.

The Revolutionary War Begins

Most representatives at the First Continental Congress hoped to reach a peaceful agreement with Britain. But Congress leaders asked each colony to raise a militia. Connecticut Sons of Liberty and others trained for battle. They hid weapons and supplies. British soldiers and Massachusetts militiamen fought at Lexington and Concord on April 19, 1775. Word spread quickly to Connecticut. Israel Putnam led 4,000 militiamen north into Massachusetts.

Connecticut militiamen gather the night before battle.

The Battle of Bunker Hill actually took place on nearby Breed's Hill.

"The Whites of Their Eyes"

The Connecticut militia joined other colonial troops at Breed's Hill outside Boston. The colonials drove back two British attacks on June 17 before running low on ammunition. Someone gave the famous order "Don't fire until you see the whites of their eyes" as the British attacked again. The colonials soon retreated. About 450 American fighters were killed or wounded. But the Battle of Bunker Hill cost the British more than 1,000 dead and injured.

Congress required agreement from all 13 colonies before it would send the declaration to King George III.

A colonial representative reads the Declaration of Independence to crowds in Philadelphia.

The Second Continental Congress met in Philadelphia in July 1775 to discuss independence and the war against Britain. Most of the representatives believed the colonies had to seek independence. They made their decision official by approving the Declaration of Independence on July 2, 1776. Connecticut eventually sent about 40,000 Connecticut residents to join the Continental army. This was about one-fifth of the colony's total population.

Gunsmiths work to create weapons for colonial soldiers.

Warehouse of the Army

Connecticut also played a major role off the battlefield. George Washington was commander in chief of the Continental army. He relied on Connecticut to supply him with blankets, clothes, food, and cannons. Every town in Connecticut provided goods for the army. Connecticut's reputation as a supply source led the British to raid Danbury on April 27, 1777. They destroyed thousands of barrels of food, 5,000 pairs of shoes, and 1,600 tents.

Connecticut's Founding Fathers

Connecticut, like all the colonies, was split between supporters of Britain and those opposed to British control. William Pitkin was a supporter of American independence. He was elected governor of Connecticut in 1766. The colony was the first one with an openly anti-British government. Connecticut's founders had a large influence on the developing young nation.

Roger Sherman

Roger Sherman was one of the major figures of the American Revolution. He helped write the Declaration of Independence. After the war he served in Congress, became mayor of New Haven, and helped rewrite Connecticut's laws.

Samuel Huntington

Samuel Huntington was known for his hard work and calm personality. He spoke out against British laws meant to punish the colonies. He was elected to the Second Continental Congress. He later served as president of the Congress. He also spent 10 years as Connecticut's governor.

Oliver Wolcott

Oliver Wolcott was too ill to sign the Declaration of Independence in the summer of 1776. Then he had to serve in the military. William Williams took his place, although Wolcott later signed the declaration. Wolcott followed Huntington as governor of Connecticut in 1796.

British troops attacked Connecticut twice in 1779. Former American officer Benedict Arnold led a British force in Connecticut on September 6, 1781. They burned most of New London before killing 80 Continentals at nearby Fort Griswold. The British surrendered six weeks later. The fighting had caused widespread damage. Farms and businesses were destroyed. The government had run up huge debts to pay for the war.

Benedict Arnold watches as fires destroy New London.

"Brother Jonathan"

Jonathan Trumbull was
the only governor to
serve both before
and after the
Revolutionary War.
He took part
in the fight for
independence along
with his four sons.
In 1775, Trumbull
had refused to help the
British after the early battles
in Massachusetts. Washington
trusted Trumbull to provide supplies
for his troops during the war.
Washington's nickname for Trumbull
was Brother Jonathan. This soon
became the name of an Uncle Sam–
like character meant to represent
all Americans.

Trumbull was
the only royal
governor to
support the
colonists over
the British.

The victorious Americans needed a new constitution to unite its states under one set of laws. Representatives gathered to discuss the matter in Philadelphia in 1787. The proposed Constitution of the United States was given to each state to be voted on in early 1788. Connecticut representatives overwhelmingly approved it on January 9, 1788. The former colony became the fifth state of the United States. It looked to the future with high hopes for success. ★

In 1787, George Washington presided over the Constitutional Convention held in Philadelphia, Pennsylvania.

True Statistics

Year Adriaen Block visited the Quinnehtukqut River: 1614

Indian population after 1616 epidemics: 6,000 to 7,000

Population of Windsor after first year of settlement: 100

Connecticut's settler population in 1670: 20,000

Number of rooms in a Connecticut schoolhouse: 1

Number of Connecticut troops led to Massachusetts by Israel Putnam: 4,000

Number of Connecticut citizens fighting in the Revolutionary War: 40,000

Number of shoes destroyed in the Danbury raid: 5,000 pairs

Did you find the truth?

T Connecticut wrote a constitution as early as 1639.

F Everyone in Connecticut agreed to fight the Revolutionary War against Britain.

Resources

Books

Dubois, Muriel L. *The Connecticut Colony.* Mankato, MN: Capstone, 2006.

Furgang, Kathy. *The Declaration of Independence and Roger Sherman of Connecticut.* New York: PowerKids Press, 2002.

Furstinger, Nancy. *Connecticut.* New York: Children's Press, 2009.

January, Brendan. *Colonial Life.* New York: Children's Press, 2000.

Koontz, Robin. *Connecticut: The Constitution State.* New York: PowerKids Press, 2011.

Marsh, Carole. *Connecticut Native Americans.* Peachtree City, GA: Gallopade International: 2004.

Ollhoff, Jim. *Connecticut.* Edina, MN: Checkerboard, 2010.

Organizations and Web Sites

Connecticut Historical Society

www.chs.org

Look at a collection of more than 8,000 objects and study the history of Connecticut from its colonial days to the present.

Mashantucket Pequot Museum and Research Center

www.pequotmuseum.org

Get a close look at Native American culture and history at the online home of this museum.

Places to Visit

Historic Putnam Cottage/ Knapp's Tavern

243 East Putnam Avenue
Greenwich, CT 06830
(203) 869-9697
www.putnamcottage.org
Visit the bright red, late 1600s house that was the site of a meeting between Israel Putnam and George Washington during the Revolutionary War.

Museum of Connecticut History

Connecticut State Library
231 Capitol Avenue
Hartford, CT 06106
(860) 757-6535
www.museumofcthistory.org
Study exhibits of Connecticut artifacts and learn about the oak tree where colonists hid their charter from the English.

Important Words

apprentices (uh-PREN-tis-ez) — people who learn a skill by working with an expert

charter (CHAHR-tur) — a formal document guaranteeing rights or privileges

colony (KAH-luh-nee) — an area settled by people from another country and controlled by that country

constitution (kahn-sti-TOO-shun) — the laws of a country that state the rights of the people and the powers of government

debt (DET) — money or something else that someone owes

epidemic (ep-i-DEM-ik) — an infectious disease that makes a large number of people sick at the same time

legal (LEE-guhl) — allowed by law

legislature (LEJ-is-lay-chur) — a group of people who have the power to make or change laws

militia (muh-LISH-uh) — a group of people who are trained to fight but who aren't professional soldiers

prejudice (PREJ-uh-dis) — unreasonable or unfair opinion based on a person's religion, race, or other characteristic

wigwam (WIG-wahm) — a dome-shaped house made of bark, grass, and mud placed over a wooden frame

Index

Page numbers in **bold** indicate illustrations

About the Author

Kevin Cunningham has written more than 40 books on disasters, the history of disease, Native Americans, and other topics. Cunningham lives near Chicago with his wife and young daughter.